First Footprints

FRAN ORENSTEIN

Aquitaine, Ltd.
Phoenix, Arizona

DEDICATION

For James, Susannah, Peter, and Kristen
Rachel, Aaron, Zayden and Kai.

Earth would be a barren world without you in it.

CONTENTS

THE EARLY YEARS: GLIMPSES OF CHILDHOOD IN NEW YORK

Our journeys begins at the first breath of life, the first wail, the first sensation of cold. We are thrust from the safe, liquid warmth of the womb, into the realities of life. What we do with that reality shapes us forever and sends us along a path. The destination, the journey, and how we take the final breath, is up to us. These are the reflections of a poet's journey.

PRELUDE

ENTER HERE ~

FIRST FOOTPRINTS is a book of poetry about childhood and the emerging adult. Please join me on this journey, but stay close because the path is sometimes confusing and convoluted. Oh, and everyone is welcome to walk the path, men and women, for we all share many of the same experiences and feelings. Please be on guard for debris, rock slides and sink holes, but take your time to smell the wildflowers, listen to the songbirds, and watch the golden sunsets.

The decades spanning the coming of age from child to girl to woman, mark her physically and psychically in an ever changing confluence of events coinciding and overlapping during her lifespan. Her response to the elements that conspire in this evolution of body and mind depend on the strengths imbued by childhood experiences and early adult influence, merging with her unique genetics.

Her choices are many and varied, but she is also constricted by the circumstances into which she was born. Opposites can mold, but they can also rip apart the clay: deprivation or affluence; religious fervor or enlightened belief, or no belief; convention and conservatism or leniency and liberalism all contribute to the formation of the girl to woman to elder. Self-acceptance and self-love are strong indicators of a secure and fulfilling life. The mask of self-loathing and self-hate hides in the shadow of her stronger sisters, fearful of rejection and derision.

Welcome to the emergent journey of one woman, of many women, of all women from child to adult. Take the side trips as lover, mother, and toiler. Follow the meandering path across four decades of life. No tickets necessary, for male or female, you have all been on this journey or will be.

Dr. Fran Orenstein   6/1/15

CHILDHOOD

The journey begins in childhood, where we are molded, nurtured and if given a continuous, generous dose love, emerge as whole human beings ready to continue and deal with the roadblocks.

FANTASTICAL FANTASIES

A child gazes from the arching bridge
at gurgling water bubbling over the rocks.
The sunlight, shining through the leafy tree,
ripples in rainbows of color on the surface.

Childhood dreams imagine
angel wings and fairy dust,
unicorns and magic swords,
mystical wizards in peaked caps.

Childhood dreams imagine
great ships unfurling sails
and pirates, sabers in hand,
swinging out over the roiling sea.

Childhood dreams imagine
a brave prince riding to rescue
the enchanted princess from
a dragon breathing red flames.

In the charmed world of childhood
magical moments of mystery abound
that only the child sees in the stream below,
safe in the fantastical world of the very young.

BROWNSTONES OF BROOKLYN

Seen from the end of the street
an endless array of sameness
stone sentinels shoulder to shoulder
proudly line the sidewalks

Brownstone houses sporting stoops
and steep stone steps
low stone walls guarding the entry
made for sitting on in summer

Playing stoop ball…smack against the steps
watching for the ice cream man
chalked potsy boxes on the sidewalk
girls bouncing balls, "A, my name is…."

Grandmothers knitting in the sun
Grandfathers greeting cronies
Kids listening as mothers gossip,
pretending not to pay attention

Brownstones with rounded turrets
heavy wooden front doors
guarding the tunnels of rooms
running front to back

Brooklyn brownstones
like pairs of identical twins
alike, but subtly different
mirroring the people who lived inside

THE COAL CELLAR

It lurks patiently,
    hiding, waiting, watching
behind the pile of coal spilling from
    beneath the creaky wooden stairs.

No windows here.
    Darkness without shadows,
bereft of light and lightness,
    flat, matte black.

Death above the stairs;
    mourning shrouding life.
She would come no more
    to fill the coal scuttle.

There are others, though.
    Giggling, fearful, small others,
seeking the sunshine door
    to the garden of roses.

Anticipating their return,
    for the rush of terror power,
Small, tremulous eyes seeking absent light
    in the cellar's blackness.

Fearful glances at the hill of coal
    At shadows dancing on stone walls
In the faint light of the open door
    Atop the creaky wooden stairs.

Fran Orenstein

7

At last…squealing door, squeaking steps
        tiny voices – hurry, hurry!
Heavy footsteps, light footsteps
            rushing past the coal hill.

It rises in anticipation, gray against gray walls.
        No one hears its soundless call.
They have opened the cellar door,
        running into the light of the rose garden.

It sinks behind the hill of coal.
        Vanquished now by sunlight,
it waits once more for darkness
        and a victim of terror.

BUBBE'S GARDEN

Bubbe lived in a brownstone in Brooklyn
Where her five children were born and raised
The day her young husband died
It's where she retreated from the world

In twenty or so years she would die there
In the room with the piano
They said cancer, but probably loneliness
Despair at the way her life turned out

The front windows gazed at an ugly factory
The back looked out on Bubbe's garden
A bower of seven sisters roses draped across a trellis
Hovered over a bench, where one could dream

An oasis in a desert of concrete and city noise
Bubbe's garden became a playground for her
grandchildren
A retreat for her daughters to talk away from the kids
A microcosm of nature seen through the kitchen window

Accessed only by a door at the far end of the dark and
scary cellar
Bubbe's garden beckoned to the grandchild brave enough
To navigate the shadowy corners and crannies
And open the door to lush red roses dripping from the
arbor

Fran Orenstein
9

CONEY ISLAND—NINETEEN FORTIES

Salty surf lapping against the beach
Hot sand sifting between burning toes
Blanketing the steps rising to
The rough wooden planks of the boardwalk

Unforgettable landmarks
The Half Moon Hotel
Its domed roof silhouetted against
The skyline and the Parachute jump

The mighty Steeplechase
Fake horses racing on elevated tracks
Screaming riders holding on for dear life
Thrilling in the excitement

And the smell, the ever present smell
Nathan's hot dogs and French fries
cotton candy, soda and ice cream
Ambrosia of the gods.

The avenues marked the Island
Surf, Mermaid and Neptune
Crossed by numbered streets
In a perfectly aligned grid

The El rumbled down Coney Island Avenue
To the end of the tracks
"Last Stop Coney Island,

Everybody off!"

Descending the stairs to beach or boardwalk or
The open trolley/train rambling noisily down
The single track between the boardwalk and Surf Avenue
The way home from a day in the City

And Seagate at the end of the peninsula
Where the elite lived behind gates
 Breathing the same salty, fishy air
As those of us who lived in the homes to the east.

REMEMBERING RICHARD THE MONSTER— CONEY ISLAND 1946

Remember Richard the Monster, the boy next door.
Remember his stuck out ears, and his spiky brown hair.
Remember his tiny, squinty eyes, and the mouth that never smiled.
Remember his screeching voice.

Remember Richard the Monster who hid behind the fence.
Remember how he jumped out and screamed.
Remember the tight band around my throat.
Remember no breath, sour spit.

Remember the pain of his punch on my arm.
Remember the sharp pain in my stomach.
Remember the shaking terror of riding past his house on my tricycle.
Remember peddling so fast I thought I would tip over.

Remember thinking six-year old thoughts.
Remember sitting on my tricycle at the gate,
Remember looking left toward Richard the Monster's house.
Remember pedaling furiously the other way.

Remember how sweet the air smelled to the right.

THE BRONX, NY – 1947 to 1952

Apartment houses brick red to yellow tan
flowed downward from the Grand Concourse
hills at forty-five degrees angles
great for sledding in winter

Treacherous to homebound commuters
slipping and sliding in winter,
hanging onto the sides of the buildings
to slow the increasing momentum

A thrill for a child's nose, pressed against
the window

Hills so steep that parked cars slid
out of their spaces and descended
faster and faster until they hit the bottom
and whatever might be in the way

Wide and elegant, the Grand Concourse
split the Bronx like a white line of scalp
parting the waves of hair
cascading down a woman's shoulders

The Yankee Stadium stood as a beacon
for diehard baseball fans
awed by the amazing feats
of Joe, Mickey, and Roger

Fran Orenstein
13

The secret heroes of boys, the secret
fantasies of girls

Sneaking into Yankee games under the turnstiles
guards turning a blind eye to a couple of kids
starting at the top of the bleachers
moving down to seats behind the dugout

The Stadium dominated the west side
under the El of the IRT subway
where travelers could sneak a peak at the game
from the elevated station at 161st. street

The train rattled into the station
they looked wistfully behind
before stepping on board to the City
their minds still sitting in the bleachers

While reality beckoned with unsheathed claws

The famous Bronx Zoo
home to the first platypus, and
lines of parents and kids,
like me, who stared in amazement

The famed Botanical Gardens
an oasis of riotous color
amid the looming darkness of apartments
respite for a soul starving for nature

We roamed the Bronx
walking across the G W Bridge
munching on sour kosher pickles

First Footprints
14

licking sweet Charlotte Rousses

The apartment building is gone
a parking lot of broken concrete and weeds
the Grand Concourse is no longer grand
now they are tearing down Yankee Stadium

Is nothing sacred in this world?

THE CREATURE

The Bronx Zoo famous for exotica
And its immense [to a child] size
And for a wonderful day out with mom
Exploring the natural world

In 1947, Australia sent the us a present
A strange creature never before seen
By anyone in this country
And it came to my Bronx Zoo

Mom and I got on the bus and traveled up
To the north Bronx to stand in a never-ending line
Mom exasperated by impatient fidgeting
And innumerable questions

At last we arrived at the longest fish tank
These young eyes had ever seen
Swimming in and out of the grasses and plants
A furry creature paddled up and down

The sign said, "Duck-billed Platypus"
It looked like somebody flattened a brown beaver
And glued on a huge duck's bill
"Native to Australia" Where's Australia?

Such was a child's introduction to the Platypus
An experience never forgotten
After nearly seven decades
And glowing memories of the Bronx Zoo

MAROON MEMORIES

Carpeting, maroon, thick and soft
Carpet sweeper, maroon on maroon
Shrieks of glee from the child riding
Across the maroon floorscape

Fresh beets wearing maroon skins
Boiled away into a maroon lake
Bobbing rocks of new potatoes surround
The white sour cream island

Old Mercury sedan circa 1950
Maroon finish edged in gleaming chrome
Fins like a maroon shark
Sliding through the streets of New York

Rugs and sweepers
Beets and borscht
Sleek shark-like cars
Maroon memories of childhood

THE WURTSBORO HILL–1940's

The day after school ends in New York City,
Cars span the George Washington Bridge.
A mass exodus of families running from heat and polio
To the cool, woodland Catskill Mountains.

Cars trail like wagon trains
To tiny bungalow colonies
Nestled between small towns and cities
Under the protective crags of the Catskills.

As the mountain range appears in the distance
Along Route 17, past the Red Apple Rest Stop
The road slowly rises,
Long and gradual, deceptive and deadly.

A dreaded, demon stretch of road
Destined to cull the weak
And reduce even the strongest cars to smoking hulks
Dying along the shoulders.

Wheezing and groaning
Car after car toils up the hill
Many dropping like dead autumn leaves
Left behind as the persistent survivors plod on.

Rejoicing when our car attains the crest
Unscathed by overheated radiator or tired transmission.
Daddy honks the horn in triumph.
Once more, we survived the Wurtsboro Hill.

GREENFIELD PARK, NY 1948-1951

Nestled beneath burnt sienna mountains,
laced with lush purple lilacs and tall verdant trees,
Greenfield Park is a blink on NY Route 52
caught in a crossroad somewhere
between Ellenville and Woodbridge.

No bandstand honors its presence.
Its non-existent streets boast no general store, or post
office.
    Barren in winter, it opens warm, summer arms to city
    dwellers, seeking solace from the trapped heat of
apartments,
        the melting tar of streets, steaming asphalt, and polio,
        finding refuge in tiny ramshackle bungalows.

When the June calendar page finally ends,
caravans of cars and busses huff and puff across the
George Washington
Bridge onto Route 17, straining up the Wurtsboro Hill
    trying vainly to crest the top, and reach the rolling
Catskill Mountains
    on the other side. Smoking cars litter the side of the
road,
        like savaged wagon trains headed west, sans oxen..

Days gloried by twittering, buzzing symphonies
Energizing the soul to revive with each rising sun.
Dusk, and I am lulled by creek-side croaking

Fran Orenstein
19

and the snick, snick of cricket feet rubbing away the dust of day.

I wish I could return to Greenfield Park,
and crawl inside the ancient lilac with a Nancy Drew mystery,
or push back and forth on the rope swing hanging from the leafless ghost tree,
counting stars, writing poems in my head,
and watching the strange lights of a round disk as it hovers,
and swiftly soars, judging this child unworthy of space travel.

But dreams of yesterday are simply dreams
lurking in the corners of reality,
testing the veracity of Grandma waving an ax,
her ever present flowered apron flapping,
as she vainly chases the chicken around the yard,
when she would only have cooked Kosher chicken, anyway,
so my Aunt Molly said, but I remember grandma-love,
the odor of chicken fat and cleanser, emanating from her apron..

Aunt Molly washing my cousin Freddy's skunky dog, Smoky, in Campbell's tomato juice, in July, 1949, pulling porcupine quills out of his nose a week later.
Smokey the musical mutt, standing on short hind legs, his black nose pushed into Freddy's clarinet, howling discordant notes,
creating a Strindberg duet, chalk on a blackboard.

Polio, closing the doors to adventure.

To boot, an escaped prisoner lurking somewhere in
the dense forest.

But immortal at twelve, I sneak off to a hotel with the
older kids,

dragging my younger cousin along, conspirators.

We crawl back, humiliated two hours later

in the custody of hulking, hideous John the
Handyman.

I swing my leather Garrison belt, its metal buckle
glinting in the flashlight beams,

shaking down the black ribbon of road.

So brave, so terrified, at the mercy of unseen
murderers.

I gained a new respect for John the Handyman that
night

A gentle soul trapped in Frankenstein's Monster,
minus the neck screws.

Growing up began with a realization of mortality,

of possibilities too frightful to ponder,

and childhood left at the roadside, languishing in the
dark.

They are dust now, those grown-ups of our past.

We are the sensible, rule-makers now.

Sometimes our child peeks out for a momentary
giggle

or a burst of song, retiring quickly, lest it be ridiculed.

I exchanged the lush and verdant mountains of New
York,

for the scrubby, rocky mountains of the desert.

Fran Orenstein
21

Sometimes, though, when it rains, the fresh, fragrant air
is a time machine, to a bygone era of laughing innocence.

THE WOODEN WRAP-AROUND PORCH

Nestled in New York's Catskill Mountains,
The Claredon proudly stood in their shadow.
Two big buildings,
posing as rooming houses,
and one lonely bungalow,
set back in the field.
But in the 1940's and 50's it spelled
HAVEN for escapees from the hot, polio-infested CITY.

A deep, wooden, wrap-around porch
encircled the main house with warm open arms,
a playground for many childhood memories.
Uncle Dave's pinochle tutorial,
Vicious canasta and monopoly games,
Jacks and Pickup Sticks
under the roof that rat-a-tatted
with rain, and shook with rolling thunder.

Sunny days, we ran through the fields
splashed in the pond,
played hide-and-go-seek,
swung on the ghost tree,
or picked blueberries,
wading through patches of poison ivy.

But, inevitably, we were all trapped
by a Catskill Mountain thunder storm
on the wooden, wrap-around porch.

Fran Orenstein
23

Scratching our Calomine smeared rashes,
we performed songs and puppet shows,
our theatrical attempts enjoyed mostly by our
mothers,
   who took breaks from cracking the Mah Jong tiles
   to watch our adaptations of Broadway reviews.

Time moves inexorably forward,
and the wooden wrap-around porch,
along with the house it sheltered for a hundred years,
burned down many decades later.
It still stands stately in our memories,
the beating of rain a bass accompaniment
for young voices singing <u>Lullaby of Broadway</u>
and the crack bam of ivory tiles.

SATURDAY AFTERNOON MOVIES IN THE CATSKILLS

It's Saturday and it's raining
Glistening drops plopping on the roof
Soggy grass under black rubber boots
Squishing as we plod to the big wooden porch.

Not a fun kid's day
Nothing to do day
Boring day.
Another game of cards?

Mothers save the day
We'll go into town to the movies.
Daddies will drive all the kids
Pick us up again.

Movies in the 1940's,
A special feature movie
Another not so special feature movie
A newsreel, and a cartoon.

The smell of wet clothes.
The scent of popcorn and melting chocolate
Fizzy cherry cokes going up our noses
Giggling, pushing, punching, shushing.

25 cents well spent
To keep us happy

Fran Orenstein

On a rainy Saturday afternoon
In the Catskill Mountains.

CATSKILL TEA PARTY

When I was eight or maybe nine
friends and dolls
Would party on the grass
Beneath the mountains

Acorn cups and leaf plates filled
with tiny pods of plants
red berries, flower petals
and miniscule pebbles

We gorged until bursting
on organic natural food
Edible of course
only in a child's imagination.

Bare silver trunk glows
Stark silhouette in moonlight
Leafless, lifeless death

(Haiku)

Previously Published in *Tales of the Supernatural*
Edited by Deborah Simpson, 2009

BIG JOHN

We kids all feared Big John
The handyman…monstrous,
ugly, huge and silent.
A scary part of our daily lives.

His stone statue face loomed over us now.
Its oversize features never revealing
the anger extruding from his pores.
Dispatched to bring us home.

Stupid smartass kids breaking the rules,
stranded, scared, subdued.
Sending Big John was the punishment;
towed home by something more terrifying.

Big John's flashlight flickered,
the sole illumination in this
black shrouded landscape,
keeping the boogie man at bay.

He might be out there lurking somewhere
hidden in the trees, a shadowy form…
the escaped murderer we heard about.
But…defiant kids determined to be free…

He swung the flashlight back and forth
I swung my heavy buckled belt
The stomp of Big John's boots accompanying
Rustling trees and skittering critters

Fran Orenstein
29

Big John never said a word
But led us briskly along the road
Framed by the black, whispering woods
We never feared Big John again.

SMIRK

Summer anguish
Not the itch of Poison Ivy
Nor the burning of bee stings
I suffered from the smirky kid

She smirked
Not a smile
Not a grin
Not even a dimple

She smirked when she won a game
She smirked when she won a fight
She ganged up on me with the other kids
And she smirked

She tattled on me
And smirked
She blamed me
And smirked

When I got smacked
A lot
And wouldn't cry
She smirked

Miss pretty as a rose
Sweet as a chocolate chip cookie
But, I know what she really was inside
A SMIRKER.

Fran Orenstein
31

FROGS

I hate frogs
    Slimy, ugly, amphibians
  Leaping at me
When I least expect it.

Summers in the Catskill Mountains
  Boy joy…scaring sissy girls
And a pond filled with fat, disgusting frogs
    Scarred for life.

They sneak up
Thrusting a slippery, frog down my back,
    Screaming, I jump around to get free
While the boys laugh themselves sick.

Cold.
  Wet.
    Wriggly.
      Disgusting.

I shriek
They laugh harder
    They push another frog in my face
I shriek louder

The frog on my back jumps free
  The boys chase me
Everyone is having a great time

Except me and the frogs.

What biologic heights attained,
A cure for cancer, a Nobel Prize?
Were I not thwarted by...
Fear of frog dissection.

STICKS AND STONES

They taunted her with words like cutting knives
Hey, two elephants put together
Followed Fat down the crowded street
Shouted by a bratty, brainless little kid

Fat and skinny had a race, and you know what
happened
Fat fell down and broke her bloated face
Could not make the broad jump in gym class
She failed every time and they all laughed

At ten she went to a costume party
Mother had a brilliant brainstorm
You can be Fanny Brice as Baby Snooks
Fat had a terrific singing voice, buried in obesity

Costumed in a short ruffled blue dress
Baring fat arms and legs to the world
Big bow in Fat's hair and stupid socks
She hated it, refused to go, fell on deaf ears.

Fat had a boyfriend in the group
There she was in all her ridiculous glory
Humiliation vied with shame
Fat's ego died, then, and no body cared

Sticks and stones will break your bones
Words will never hurt you

Invisible fractures of self-esteem
Mutilated self-image, festering anger

Forever wearing a sign upon her back
Here I am, Fat, kick me with words
Stab my heart and twist the phrase
Obliterate the real me that might have been

SUMMER NINETEEN FIFTY

We didn't know about visitors from space
We lived our lives in fearful innocence
Envisioning spectacular mushroom clouds
And world destruction in flaming red
      Bomb shelters
            Radioactive fallout

It simply appeared in the sky at dusk
This circular silvery disk, flashing lights
Hovering over the edge of the field
Beneath a towering Catskill mountain
      I was witness to
            An entity unknown

UFO was not a word in our vocabulary
Alien invasions happened on the movie screen
And I kept swinging, neck arched, gazing up
At something that shouldn't be there
      But it was…there
            Hovering overhead

I gently kicked forward and back
In a monotonous arc above the grass
On the ghost tree swing, alone in my head
Writing poems of childhood fantasies
      As above me it hung
            A floating pancake

I looked up and felt no fear, but wonder
It looked down at the lonely girl on the swing
We observed each other the Visitors and I
In the quietude of a Catskill Mountain evening
　　　No fear or concern
　　　　　A learning moment

Having decided something or other about me
It moved on into the darkening sky and disappeared
I contemplated a poem about flat, round disks
But ten-year-old angst overwhelmed the UFO
　　　Hovering over a Catskill field
　　　　　A moment lost

MORE SUMMER NINETEEN FIFTY

Some days after the hovering disk
Visited me while alone on the swing at dusk
We five laughing, screaming children
Played tag at the base of the ghost tree
    Along the grassy field

I saw them in the distance in a perfect line
One behind the other moving to the mountain
Five brown furry creatures standing upright
Like bears, but not bears, furry men
    Across the berry field

As the oldest, bravest or most foolish child
The kids followed me wherever it might lead
Beneath the barbed-wire fence onto forbidden land
Where furry bear-like men walked in a line
    Among the berry bushes

It could have been a great or dismal quest
For five fearless explorers seeking answers
Had the youngest not caught her back on a barb
Shrieking and howling like a trapped animal
    Aborting the adventure

For fifty years I made no connection
Until the obvious declared itself as truth
The five furry bear-like men surely
Crewed the silver disk that had hovered
    Above the ghost tree

HEADLIGHTS

Giggly is thirteen
Emerging pubescence,
Tumultuous, shifting moods
Physical hints of womanhood

Giggly is childlike
Teddy bear comfort
Huggy needy
Cinderella dreams

Giggly is womanly
Pink lipstick
Body hate
Budding breasts

Giggly has a crush
He's 16
Dreamy
Notice me, please

Giggly's sad awakening
He likes big boobs
Age 15
They call her Headlights.

HIGH SCHOOL 1955

Geography of New York City
Five boroughs,
Surrounded by water,
Rambling rivers, flowing narrows,
the mighty Atlantic.
High schools with swimming pools.

Proclamation of nitwits
In the event of an atomic bomb attack
You must learn to swim
      Swim where?
Across the Atlantic to Europe?
NO!
To New Jersey across the River

Enter Miss Swim Teacher extraordinaire
100 years old if a day
Clothed in a long, black, swim dress
White hair tightly bunned
Wrinkles stretched across pale, boney features.
Moving in slow motion.

She gestures to the wall, voice quivering.
Where hangs a 12 foot pole with a hook.
"Nothing to fear, I will save you with that."
Imagination runs amok
Miss Ancient Swim Teacher running alongside
The pool with a 12 foot hook.

Enter stage left, Girl, afraid of water
eyeing the hook and the ancient mariner
        Uninspiring thoughts
of incipient death by drowning.
Lined up, seven fearful neophytes
Stare helplessly at the water

        OH GOD! It's the deep end.
        Two seniors tread water, prepared for rescue
        "Jump," Miss Ancient Mariner yells.
        One by one they hesitate then jump in
        and paddle, seniors trailing at the ready.
        Until girl, afraid of water, stands at the brink.

        "Jump," Ancient Mariner shouts.
            Girl stands frozen.
        "Coward. Yellow streak down your back," she shrieks
            Is this me, Girl wonders?
        Will this determine life's path?
        Will my decision today mar tomorrow?

        Girl speculates on a life of shame.
        Girl contemplates a yellow spine.
        Hears the snickering girls on the bench,
        The angry panting of Miss Ancient Mariner.
        Girl turns and walks from the pool.
            Bombs be damned.

HIGH SCHOOL DREAMSCAPE

Paradise or purgatory
Paradox and perfidy

Acne and angst
Agony and ecstasy.

Reduced to nothingness
by selective memory and age.

Rendered meaningless
by time and experience.

Yet lingering in the soul,
bundles of unhealed wounds.

A YOUNG GIRL'S DREAMS

When she was young, she dreamed of esoteric scenes
Unearthing great discoveries in Egypt
The secret lives of ancient kings and queens
Deep within a dark and dismal crypt

Picture words inscribed upon the stone
To be deciphered in her clever, linguist's mind
Revealing mysteries of flesh and bone
Treasured jewels and golden finds

When she was young she dreamed a life absurd
Traveling the world both near and far
Respected master of the written word
Journalist, reporter, shooting star

Interviews with soldiers in the field
Scribing battle stories they could tell
Hurried conversations that would yield
Tales of women's war-time living hell

When she was young she dreamed that law
Was bloodless battles to be fought
And she, avenger in the monsters' maw
Would prosecute the evil in the court

Beneath the weight of Justice's scales
Standing there before the bench
Her heartfelt words of grim and guilty tales
Would sway them to eradicate the stench

Fran Orenstein
43

In 1956, they were just dreams
Forever unfulfilled by rules and life
By parent's hopes and secret schemes
And women's place as teacher, nurse, and wife.

THE PERFECT AGE

Eighteen is a special year
Growing up and moving on
A time when things you once held dear
Change and then are gone

Eighteen is an age of dreams
Of where life's stream will flow
Imagined plans and fancy schemes
Bear fruit and start to grow

Eighteen is the perfect age
To face each new-born day
And as you pass from stage to stage
Pause and smile along the way

Fran Orenstein
45

MATERNAL LOVE

You were my best friend
I told you everything…almost
You were my darkest enemy
I fought your need to control

We shared so many things
Like books and shoes and tales
Yet between us lay a chasm
Neither of us would ever cross

For you loved too much
Your love a depth
No child could fathom
A ribbon tying heaven and hell

Your fears blew from your nostrils
To envelop me in sticky webs
Suffocating desires and dreams
Quelling rebellion with guilt

Mired in your own dark pain
You fought for control
Warping my perceptions of love
Deciding the direction of my life

Yet I loved you beyond all reason
I turned to you in miserable need
And you, you sent me away
Forging the future you wanted for me

INDIFFERENT LOVE

Yours was the seed that designed her
And nothing more than that
Distant, indifferent, uncaring
Disinterested in a girl-child

Dreaming of the son never to be
Losing the joy of fatherhood
Within your own private hell
Of fathering a girl

Nothing she could do made up for it
Her wasted dreams of being a boy
Wishing for a link to you
Just to please an indifferent father

All those lost year, yearning
For what you could not have
Never seeing the joy of a daughter
And what she might have given you.

CONSEQUENCES

Flip a stone upon a lake,
Make a wish and it is gone
Ripples spread in widening circles
Stretching to oblivion

Drop a word into the air,
Comes a breeze and it is gone
Echoes linger ever after
Words of love, words of harm.

Drop a dream into the night
Just a flash and it is gone
Memories that one day surface
Ripples we can build upon.

Beware the things we toss away
In an instant they are gone
Remnants of the thoughts we share
Into the breeze, the air, the pond

SUMMER SOUNDS

Old memories
Invading the brain
On hot summer nights

Crickets in the grass
Car horns blaring
Hot summer sounds

Country music
City music
Through the open window

Fran Orenstein

THE EMERGING WOMAN: The Search For Enlightenment

No life forms or vegetation will be harmed if you stray
from this path unless there be dragons afoot.
Divergent roads are chosen by your individual and
instinctual selections.
Slow down at curves to avoid collisions.
Meander at your own pace, but with an eye toward
mortality.
Stop at the scenic views and watch the sun rise and
set.
Occasionally sniff the flowers and listen to the birds.
Life is a journey in beauty and peace
If you make it so.

FREEDOM

A woman walks a twisted path never knowing where the next bend leads.

In her lifetime the world has changed and impacted the many faces of her existence Technology emerging in her older years leaves her boggling at the pods,
computers, readers, and electronic devices
created to confuse everyone in her generation.

She buys an electronic gadget and the next year or the year after it is obsolete.
Now she begins to feel her own obsolescence in an ever changing world.
What started as simple radios with giant tubes and record players with scratchy needles
are now a cacophony of sounds heard through tiny ear-plugs.

When she was a young woman, she wore heels, stockings, girdles, gloves and skirts,
whatever the weather, it was mandated to be accepted, fashionable.
Today, anything goes, even body parts partially revealed, once considered shameful.
From hairstyles, to make up, to dress, to accessories, even in the workplace
all is acceptable in this new free world; slacks, leggings, jeans and shorts.

Fran Orenstein

She walks free, arms swinging, purse swinging, hair swinging, head high,
delighting in an individuality that belongs to her alone.
She is not a clone of other women and the fashionistas in current vogue.
In sneakers, sandals or five inch heels, her legs feel the breeze in naked joy.

There are choices open to her daughters that she never dreamed existed
choices to be married, single, divorced, living with a significant other
male, female, different race and culture, different beliefs.
Whatever she chooses is hers in the creation of an individualistic dream.
A life belonging just to her to meet her needs and goals and desires.

Motherhood is there in whatever lifestyle she chooses, or not.
This woman of an aging generation looks back and wonders what she would have done
had the world of today been open to her in the constricted world of the past.
Never mind, she has it now and strides forward into the next curve in the road.

METAPHOR OF LIFE

Lights dim, winking out.
The crimson velvet drapes descend,
obliterating an illusion.
The final act is ended.
There is no repeat performance.
No curtain calls.

Rousing applause fades into silence
filling the void with hollow echoes.
Where once actors walked the stage
igniting flames of creativity,
adulation is but a memory
receding into the backdrop.

Ghosts drift through the theater,
filled with hopeful expectations
and unrealistic dreams.
Daunted by the silence,
they peer at empty seats
that stare blindly into the darkness.

Renewal is waiting in the wings
Entering from stage right
With a sharp cry of joy and fear
The theater's heart beats once more
as a crescendo of applause
filled with hope, rises.

The ghosts withdraw behind the scenes

Fran Orenstein
53

observing the enactment of a fantasy
played out upon the stage,
knowing that this too shall end
when the crimson velvet curtain
falls far into the future.

THE PATH

The path of life's journey is
imbedded with stones of experience.
Each colorful step an adventure,
Every turn an expedition
into triumphs and failures
yet to be explored.

Kaleidoscopes of color blend
With myriad sounds creating
sensory invasions of chaos and peace.
Experiential joys and sorrows are
Landscapes edging the meandering
Way of life's path.

Wending over peaks invisible in the clouds
Often insurmountable
Across chasms whose boundaries are obscured
By fog and murky unknowns,
The path wanders on, infinitely patient
While we in our finite lives
Choose to follow or not.

Fran Orenstein
55

FREE TO BE ME

If I knew where I were going
     I'd be there.

If I could find the way,
     that is…

Around curves
Over mountains

Across rivers
Through deserts

Along shore lines
Wherever the roads lead

No promises in life they say,
     Of love
     peace
        joy.

Bits and pieces along the way
     Maybe…

To where ever I am going
    If I only knew where…

ALL SHE EVER DREAMED

All she ever dreamed about was motherhood
From the naked rubber dolls clutched in sticky hands
To gurgling silk-skin babies cradled in her arms
She always saw her life fulfilled by children

She wanted many children, this lonely only one
They would know laughter and rivalry
Companionship and sharing,
All the pieces of a life she never had

And when she was gone into the mist of time
They would not be alone in this world
For there would be the others or another
Genetic echoes of the dreams she dreamt

She saw her future reflected in the mirror
And the face she saw smiled back
You will be the fairest mother in the land
The voice whispered from the shiny glass

Though all her other dreams faded with time
Unfulfilled and withering into invisibility
The children existed, real and touchable
And the years of yearning were fulfilled

But time moved on and life happened
Darkness descended and fueled an anger unresolved
One day they left and turned their backs, never to return
Left her aging and alone...unloved, unwanted

Fran Orenstein
57

Now the mirror reflects a lonely soul
For she cannot fathom what forces intervened
How the dreams she so lovingly and carefully nurtured
Could burn away in the fires of anger and turn to dust

ALONE

From first lusty cry
to last rattling gasp
We walk the path alone
Encumbered only by our minds

Prisoners of thoughts
Chained to beliefs
Isolated by feelings
Barricaded behind the bars of ego

Aloneness in a world of chaos
Wandering amid the mobs
Caught in the invisible bubble
That makes each one unique

We may acquiesce
Accepting words and deeds
Imposed by other minds
Losing individuality

Perhaps we fight the norm
Set aside decisions made for us
By others less informed
Standing tall and defiant

We interact, appear engaged
In reality, we live our lives alone
Silently stepping along the path
That winds across the years

Fran Orenstein

THE ULTIMATE ACHIEVEMENT

Pursue a dream as it unfolds
Wipe the mist that clouds your eyes
      Deny the babble of voices
Assaulting your throbbing ears

Follow your intentions
      Even in wavering, quivering fear
      Place one foot before the other
Sword unsheathed, ever onward

The path will curve and bend
Turning upon itself
      Then straighten to deceive the eye
Into believing it will be easy

Fooled, you rush forward blindly
Only to collide with stone walls
      Refusing to crumble before you
And again the road takes a sharp turn

Keep the dream in sight
Push aside the obstacles
      March with resolve into the future
To your ultimate achievement.

THE SIXTIES

They were the changing times
Those days of Bob and Joan and Pete
P, P, and M serenading a lonely dragon
His sorrow provoking tears like rain

They were the years of assassinations
Of great men falling into martyrdom
And still the tide surged forward
Unstoppable even in the hail of bullets

They were hippy, happy years of flowers and love
A quartet singing of diamonds in the sky
Fueled by hallucinations and visions
Perpetuated by snorts and plungers

They were the years that changed a world
Forever remembered in books and songs
Peace symbols that still endure on ancient, rusting
VW campers driven by aging bearded men

They were the years of long hair wreathed in flowers,
Dancing barefoot in abandoned joy in a field
For a moment in time, oblivious of fear and pain
In their world beyond a Hudson River Valley farm

Previously published in The Florida State Poets
Association: Anthology 2009

Fran Orenstein
61

THE CORNER OF FREE WILL

Choices shape the journey of one's life
    as it moves on from birth to death.
Every crossroad displays a sign
    clearly marked in vibrant colors.

"This is The Corner of Free Will
    you have the choice to stop or go
To turn or move ahead or not;
    decisions made at your own risk."

The Corner of Free Will takes no responsibility
    for choices made by logical reflection,
or hasty, rash, emotion-driven thought.
    The decisions belong to the decider.

To go back and relive is not an option
    Only forward steps or stagnation is allowed
Confronting us every minute of our lives
    As we cross the Corner of Free Will, or not.

SUMMER OF LOVE

Hippie kids named her Summer Moon,
conceived in spaced-out times
of long flowery dresses
flowing over bare, sandaled feet.

Hot summer days growing up in
crowded cities like pizza ovens
towering above tar-sticky streets,
melting under the relentless sun.

Dry summer heat, mercilessly burns
the fields of wilting wildflowers
where Summer Moon's baby, Calliope
toddles away like an escaped felon.

Rockin' music blares from speakers
across the crowded meadow.
A new generation rocks to the beat
of another summer of love.

Fran Orenstein
63

THE INVISIBLE WOMAN

Who is this invisible woman
Whose voice is never heard
Whose words whistle in the wind
Or die un-noticed in the void

The muted sounds that leave her lips
Remain unheeded
The lessons she might teach
Remain unlearned

Her words suggest ideas
That crash and burn
Lost in the chaos of other voices
And she shrinks further into oblivion

She speaks but no one listens
Another voice repeats her words
The multitudes applaud and laud
A unique and brilliant thought

The answer to world peace
May pass through her lips
But no one ever hears
The invisible woman

THE AWAKENING

He breathed into her soul
Awakening a sleeping passion
      Lying dormant in the depths
            Of long forgotten memories

Buried beneath time's passage
Smothered by the crush of life
      His breath stirred a tiny spark
            Until it caught and flamed

Burning in an unfamiliar heat
Igniting feelings she thought lost
      Blood surging to places withered
            In a long and frozen slumber

He breathed into her soul
Returning her misplaced life
      Like a lost and frightened child
            At last, tucked safely in her bed

Previously published in *Ethereal Erotica,* a poetry
anthology
Edited by Deborah Simpson, 2010

THE LATTICE OF LOVE

A passionate, lusting physicality
    Satisfying libidinous urges
To thrust the human psyche
    Into a climax of its most powerful quest

A magnetic attraction of opposites
    Resolved to move the other
Into a circle of familiarity
    Each pulling and pushing to no avail

A gentle drifting of like beings
    Toward a melding of selves
Blended into a single organism
    Carefully nurturing the bond

A respect of human diversity
    Accepting passion and friendship
Entwining lust and tenderness
    Creating an impenetrable lattice of love

Previously published in Ethereal Erotica, an anthology
edited by
    Deborah Simpson, 2010

THE RIFT

They seek to heal the rift between them
The jagged crack wending its way beneath their feet
One on one side, one on
the other, separating
Hands held, slipping, fingers touching, slipping

The fissure widens, rending them apart
Their minds growing further adrift
And love slips silently into the
crevasse
Lost to brief glimpses of distant memories

Separated by space and eroding time
They watch the years drift on, and wonder
In unexplained, bewildered
anger where it went
This love they once held sacred, mislaid

They will meet again in some future time
Unknowing that the rift they watched in this life
Follows throughout
eternity, always waiting
For the glue of healing love they both possess

Fran Orenstein
67

LOVE LOST

At seventeen love squeezed her heart
Until breath came in small gasps
All reason fled her mind
And she saw only him

At eighteen she climbed love's peaks
And stood at the summit of joy
Lifted to the greatest heights
And she saw only him

At nineteen in white gown and veil
She vowed to love forever
To care and share her life
And she saw only him

At nineteen love shattered with deceit
And cruel words, with mental anguish
But still she lingered in this travesty
And she saw only him

At thirty-two, she knew the dream was lost
In the chilly darkness of unrequited love
But by then there were the children
And she saw the real him

At thirty-seven, she severed ties and bled
From eighteen years of misery
Saved only by the children
And she saw him in them

As her life moves inexorably to the end
Love is buried in an avalanche of distrust
From which she cannot dig a tunnel
And retrieve the memory of love

Fran Orenstein

THE MIRROR OF DUALITY

The crack appears one day
in an upper corner of the mirror
spreading diagonally.
As days become years,
it zigzags downward,
a jagged schism in the glass.

Left reflecting inner vibrant youth.
Right imaging life's true design.
Always split, like the earth
opened by a fractured fault,
Undulating in a dance of destiny.
        Daring muted by wisdom.

Left never ages,
forever young with dreams
and expectations
      invincible, indestructible,
it forges forth into love,
      open to life's offerings.

Left, ever alive and vibrant,
plunges into adventure,
excited by new ideas,
filled with plans and aspirations,
attitude, optimism and idealism,
      flaunting passion.

Life wanders through time

Slowly at first…then…
quickening with the expanding rupture
        dividing youth and age
until the rift exceeds the span of a step
        and an arched bridge arises.

Right contemplates,
growing wise and knowing,
filled with memories
tempered by experiences,
wounded by the slivered shards
        of love and rejection.

Right reflects streaks of gray
wrinkles and brown spots on aging skin
thickening hips and drooping breasts
hanging skin no longer firm and taught,
flabby jowls bracketing extra chins.
        Fearful of love's possibilities.

Visions on the right of slower gait,
perhaps a faint limp,
shaky, arthritic hands,
stiff knees and aching back,
clouded eyes squinting through a mustard haze
        seeking one last escapade.

Left fights to exist, to grow
        to keep ideas alive and thriving.
Life is an adventure
        Live life and live on
Keep the magic going one more day
        Love and be loved.

                    Fran Orenstein
                    71

Too soon, the mirror fogs
The schism closes, images fade
like the last vestiges of light at sunset.
        The cycle is complete and
both sides merge into the mist of eternity
            joined in spirit.

THE SOUL MIRROR

Gazing from the mirror,
intense eyes bore into her soul,
        opening a portal to a lonely spirit,
                bereft of love,
                        rejected, and invisible.

Smokey clouds obscure
the blue infinity of possibilities,
        framing the fragile tree of life,
                its arms draped in lacy green,
                        ready to embrace.

One red flower, pulsing with love
teases from the highest branch,
        unreachable, except by eagles
                or an open heart gasping, grasping,
                        reaching for passion.

The final choice
        before frost's withering sting
                drives life's blood to eternal dust
                        still time to choose!
                        Her eyes spark and glint.

Her eagle spirit soars to the realm of possibilities,
                to grasp the one red flower in its talon
                        voiding the loneliness,
                                returning her soul to joy.

Fran Orenstein
73

Like an Eagle, she
will fly.

Previously published in *The Love and Romance Poetry Anthology*
Edited by Deborah Simpson, 2009

THE MIRROR OF TRUTH

Behind the mirror of truth,
Beauty lurks, a furtive shadow
edging around the corner.
"See me, hear me, love me,"
she whispers, slipping back
into obscure safety.

"I am lovable, I am , I am."
The beauty shadow cries silently
into the darkness.
Who hears the tiny cry?
An empty void.

Gentle, lovable, beauty shadow sighs.
A tentative step, then another
and another, and another,
faster and faster,
breath rasping, arms flailing,
to the top of the hill.

She throws back her head,
spreads her arms to the universe
and screams,
"I am a beautiful, lovable, gentle woman."
Out of the void a million voices cry out,
"Yes, you are."

Previously published in *The Love and Romance Poetry Anthology,* Edited by Deborah Simpson, 2009

Fran Orenstein

THE MIRRORS ON HER WALL

There are mirrors on her wall,
    two-dimensional images
without depth or passion,
    hiding reality…

The courageous warrior, bearing battle scars
Some won
    Some lost
        Some unresolved

The powerful woman, imbued with strength
Determined
    enduring
        tenacious in beliefs

The needy woman, craving affection
Vulnerable
    fearful
        anticipating rejection

The passionate woman, sensual and sexy
Warm
    loving
        loyal in friendship

The bright woman, funny and playful
Mischievous
    gamester
        giggling child

There are many mirrors on her wall,
    reflections of her soul.
Multi-dimensional roles
    she may choose to reveal
        or not.

Previously published in *The Love and Romance Poetry Anthology*
Edited by Deborah Simpson, 2009
Florida State American Association of University Women Poetry Contest, 2007-2008
Free Verse Second Place

THE APOCALYPSE

Her heart beats on despite the momentary terror
A gasp restores a breath the brain forgot
Momentary silence assaults deafened ears until
Survival snaps its fingers and the din of life surfaces

Reality thrusts an icy finger down her spine
The past spins in a dizzying vortex of memory
A thick gray fog masks future dreams
The present takes center stage obscuring all else

One word delivers the final stroke of doom
To a life unfinished in this time-line
Accomplishments yet to be explored
Laughter, tears, joy, sorrow, love and loss

So many questions yet unanswered, left dangling
Amid the projects half-done, the wishes unfulfilled
Promises yet to be delivered, gifts unsent
Blackness descends for a finite moment in time

A vibrant life derailed by a single word
Uttered by a dispassionate voice in a white jacket
"I'm sorry to tell you, but the tumor is…malignant!"
The brain shuts down and the heart appears to stop

Or so it seemed at that apocalyptic moment in time
Yet twenty years and more have passed and
Her heart still pumps nectar through her body
Feeding a brain that yet has promises to keep.

TRIBUTE AFTER CANCER

I live in you this time around
a gift from the God Spirit
Strong, swift to fly in danger
Shelter in pain and adversity
A cocoon for the butterfly within

Pleasures and passion in senses
Sensual in passions and pleasure

Bearing children in great pain
Comforting their pain
With broad lap and strong arms
Sweet kisses and gentle words
A cocoon for their butterflies

Perfect and imperfect
You are what you are

Reality is a mirror
Acceptance is reality
A spiritual lesson this lifetime
Before you turn to dust

I live in you
There is nowhere else

Fran Orenstein
79

THE RESOLUTION

Awareness grows in the brain
of invading change.
Amidst a revelation of revolution,
it stockpiles responses.

Slowly processing discordant notes
raging with established behaviors,
the mind seek peaceful resolution
to a mental revolution

Promises of change
inspire disobedience
engendering upheaval
and psychic chaos.

Impending corruption
encouraged by non-compliance,
promotes hypocrisy
and delivers nothing.

Raising barriers to transformation,
crushing the power of will,
reinstalling acceptable modalities,
gray matter signs a peace treaty
ending the revolt

The mind rests.
when chaos sleeps
and balance is restored.

Calm reemerges.
Hail the power of chocolate

THE GIRL-CHILD

Drifting through misty clouds
Disembodied voices
     Wake up!

Unfocused white caps bobbing
Fuzzy, distant voices
     Wake up!

Gleaming steel, blinding lights
Clearer, insistent voices
     Wake up!

IT'S A GIRL!

Exploding stars
Cheering crowds for
My daughter

Somewhere along the path
We misplaced love.
Friendship tripped and fell on
Sharp pebbles, scraping its knees

Love hid quietly
Rooting as a sturdy oak
Towering over the path of mistrust
Memories like drooping Spanish Moss

Under the tree

Nestled in the silent shade
Seedling reflections of a beloved girl-child
Lie buried in the roots

Awaiting love's emergence
to rise and bloom
Healing the wounds
So friendship may grow tall

Fran Orenstein

THE PICTURES ON HER WALL

These are the pictures in her room:
Horses, necks bowed in dry grass
inside fences with invisible gates.
Serious women, eyes turned toward
unrevealed futures, unattainable.
Photos of cherished children who belong to another.

And this is what she does:
She arises to a job unloved.
At night, she shares her space with a flickering box,
or the cat, an indifferent lover.
She flips through the pages of others' adventures,
The phone, her connection to the world,
yet hated for its disconnection.

This is where she goes
She shops for new beginnings that never happen,
and spends Saturday night at the movies with girlfriends.
She awakens to a hollow Sunday, alone with the cat,
again.
She flies thousands of miles to see the children,
who aren't hers, unable to let go of remembered love,
yet refusing to acknowledge the yearning of her womb-
heart.

And this is what she knows:
Change is wandering, lost in a hall of mirrors.
Rhett Butler will never carry her up the stairs.
Passion is for the Scarletts of this world.

Her existence is too dark to write the poetry
hidden behind her eyes.
The wings of life rush past her,
beating her into the earth.
The pulses of her womb-heart grow fainter.

Florida State Poets Association Poetry Contest, 2011
Third Place

A LETTER TO MY DAUGHTER

Who were you, oh beautiful child of my womb?
Rockets and stars exploding in a delivery room
Were fears of loud noises grounded then in your tiny ears
No one else blinked
No one else flinched
Were we the lone witnesses to Fourth of July in March

Or was it an illusion

They made me go to sleep
Forced the mask over my face
You were on the edge of emergence
I never heard your first cry
Missed it all
Suckered into sleep

No female power then

What were you? Screaming with colic 12 hours a day
Allergic to formulas, diapers, baby oils
Fearful of water, though you floated peacefully for nine
months
Crying, crying, crying
No sleep, no rest, nerves flayed raw
I shuddered at the sound of baby cries

Not your fault

And you, dearest daughter, immersed in infant innocence

No intimation of the chaos you perpetrated
When at peace, smiling in perfect beauty
Thick black hair, growing longer every day
I envisioned it molting
Spread over the crib by dawn

Never happened

Blue eyes, turning aquamarine at eighteen
For some inexplicable reason
Brilliant child, able in all the arts
Disinterested in any arts
Except writing and poetry
Awards and publishing at sixteen

Suddenly giving up

Now educated, talented, a feminist
Perhaps one day the world
Will be enchanted and altered
By your poetry or prose
Should you choose to share it

Please

Fran Orenstein

THE PIANIST'S HANDS–A SONNET TO MY SON

Flexed in graceful arcs, they pause and hover
Awaiting downward strokes of the baton
Arched like trembling hands of someone's lover
At last the cue and they are called upon

To plunge into the depths of passion's song
They crash in strident chords then babbling rills
Delicious harmony both soft and strong
Notes climbing high in rising warbling trills

The left hand thrust into the booming sound
Of bass notes' pulsing, thrumming, background beat
As right hand leads the way to softer ground
Together playing deep and full and sweet

Hand over hand, flying fingers flee
Scaling the ivories C to C to C

The First Meeting

First seen through prisms of sparkling glass
As they wheeled me past the nursery
Tiny bow in his wispy hair standing straight up
Perfect miniscule face in the peaceful repose of the
just born.

Rosy cheeks like chipmunk jowls
Surrounding a pursed rosebud mouth
Eyes closed against the glaring light
Body swaddled like a cocoon

And I, I fell instantly in love, a love
That rushed in like a great infusion of blood,
filling my pulsing, needy heart.
I knew at last what love really meant

The Second Meeting

She thundered down the hall
"Babies a' comin', babies a' comin'."
This jolly nurse with the round chocolate features
And the never-ending smile.

She handed him to me and his eyes opened
He looked up at the light and turned his head
Then dropped to my face and stared
And I knew he defied the laws of newborns

Fran Orenstein

I unwrapped his tiny body and checked the parts
Every toe and finger in place
Peering in the diaper, that too
His eyes never left my face, imprinting

This was what motherhood was about
This bonding with the first born
The one who would love me like no other
Until time and fate ripped our love apart

UNRAVELING

Fragile stitches binding us
The child I loved above all else
The first-born, beloved, adored
A living childhood dream

A flicker of hope amid chaotic
Times of joy and sadness
Volatile teen years now ashes
A young man of quality rising

Leaving on your quest
To follow your dreams
A hug and whispered words
"I don't think I'll be coming back."

Tears hung behind my lashes
Train doors slid together in finality
And all I heard was the rattle
Of wheels growing fainter

You met your love out there
Her name, her voice, her face
Mysteries ripping apart the
Fragile stitches of our lives

A new focus in your secret world
As it has and always will be
Mothers, the givers of life
Fade into the shadowed past

Fran Orenstein

THINGS LEFT BEHIND

They leave things behind
The flotsam and jetsam of childhood
The unwanted, discarded memories
That once formed the center of their world

They leave things behind
Family, home, stuff tossed in the trash
The only things left to remember
Are pictures like slides in the mind

They leave things behind
Only to return and leave again
Saying finally *I don't think I'll be back*
Waving from the car or train or plane

They leave things behind
Lonely mothers left with nothing
But yellowing pictures in tattered albums
Of soft sweet red-cheeked babies

They leave things behind
Forgotten like the toys of childhood
Perhaps a phone call here and there or not
Hi Mom, gotta go, talk to you soon

They leave things behind
Just as it was meant to be through time
Life cycles moving inexorably forward
It will happen to them one day.

First Footprints

OBSOLESCENCE

When did your heart close
Gentle man
When did your serenity fade away
Patient man

You do not see these wrinkling eyes
The graying hair, the slower walk
The mind that takes a little longer
To assimilate and comprehend

A world to which it was not born
A complicated world
Of strange terms and devices
An alien world, no longer simple

Forward thirty years
A new age has emerged
Your son understands
And you do not

Will his impatience pierce your heart
Cause your eyes to tear
At the frustration in his voice
Perhaps you will remember today

When technology was simple
And you understood...

Fran Orenstein

REMEMBERING THE FIRST TIME

Separated by time and distance
Two generations meet for the first time
A tiny pink hand curled
Around an wrinkled aged finger
    Eyes lock in understanding
Joining this tiny infant to me
I am your Grandmother
I will love you forever and ever

CHILDREN OF THE LIGHT

They are the babies of our babies
The children of the light
The crystal children sent
To save this world.

They heal our souls and bodies
With loving joy and peace
Bright eyes filled with love
Smiles endearing

They lead us on the road
To enlightened understanding
Of the future that waits
To be reclaimed

They are the special children
Babies of our babies
Who bring us light from darkness
And open the gates of peace

Fran Orenstein

A SPECIAL LOVE

Your miniature hand clasps my finger
Binding my pulse to yours forever

Your tiny eyes bore through mine
Reading into my needy soul

Love grips my heart
With squeezing tentacles

Draining my mind of all thought
Save you, my first-born grandchild

So shall you live in me
And I shall live in you

Until we both fade away into dust
Then meet again as spirits

Forever more

NOTE FROM THE AUTHOR

The journey to enlightenment and fulfillment continues in Winding Ways, but it does not end there. Join me on the second journey, but remember, thar be dragons, so maintain vigilance.

Dr. Fran Orenstein June, 1, 2015

Thanks for reading my book. If you enjoyed it, please take a moment to leave me a review at your favorite online-retailer.

Connect with me on Social Sites

Twitter: https://twitter.com/Hubysmom
Facebook: https://www.facebook.com/fran.orenstein.1
LinkedIn: https://www.linkedin.com/pub/dr-fran-orenstein/1b/278/295
Website: http://www.franorenstein.com

Discover other titles by Fran Orenstein

Adult Novels
Danse Macabre
Death in D Minor
Murder in Duplicate
Gaia's Gift

Chapter Books
Amber and the Whipped-Cream Dress
One Amber Too Many

'Tween Books
Fat Girls From Outer Space
The Shadow Boy Mysteries, a Trilogy

Young Adult
The Book of Mysteries, a Single-Volume Series
The Calling of the Flute
The Spice Trader's Daughter

Poetry
Reflections (Out of Print)
Five Six Pick Up Sticks (Out of Print)

First Footprints

ABOUT THE AUTHOR

Fran Orenstein, Ed.D., is the award-winning author of novels, short stories, and poetry for kids, 'tweens, teens, and adults. She wrote her first poem at age eight and submitted a short story to a magazine at age twelve. Fran has been a teacher, written professionally as a magazine editor/writer, counseled people with disabilities, and also wrote political speeches, newsletters, legislation, and promotional material while working for New Jersey State Government for twenty-two years.

She has published academically, and written professional papers on gender equity and violence prevention, which she presented at national and international conferences. Fran managed programs for women in gender equity, childcare, and disabilities, as well as serving as Special Projects and Disabilities Officer for the AmeriCorps Commission in New Jersey.

Fran has a BA in Early Childhood Education, a MEd in Counseling Psychology, and an Ed.D. in Child and Youth Studies.

She especially loves writing for kids and teens, and considers her children and grandchildren her best inspiration.

All Fran's books are available at on-line bookstores in EBook and paperback format.